DR. DEBORAH J. CLAXTON

THE WONDERS
of Widowhood

GOD'S "GOTCHA" COVERED!

THE WONDERS OF WIDOWHOOD
God's "Gotcha" Covered

Published by
Kingdom Publishing, LLC
Odenton, Maryland, U.S.A.

Printed in the U.S.A.

Paperback ISBN: 978-1-947741-69-0

THE WONDERS OF WIDOWHOOD
GOD'S "GOTCHA" COVERED

TABLE OF CONTENT

Acknowledgements

I want to devote this book to the memory of all my comrades, associates, and fellow-laborers in the gospel who have had a spouse who has departed in death. They are too numerous for me to call them all by name. I give special acknowledgement to my family members, especially to those who have died in faith and in the faith. (Heb. 11: 39).

I dedicate this book in remembrance of multitudes of friends and acquaintances who have influenced my life in Christ, now living and/or deceased. They also are too numerous for me to call them all by name.

I especially want to dedicate this book to my sister, Lenora, in memory of her late husband, Deacon Paul F. Showell. His life stands as a memorial of encouragement to me, and I learned, to so many others as well. It was at the time of his homegoing that I discovered that the words, **"WRITE THE BOOK"** had been repeated to so many of his acquaintances. I thought that it was a prophetic word that he was giving to me to complete this book that I had started. Often when we talked, our conversation ended with Paul repeating those same words. Somehow, the last time we had a conversation, and he repeated those words, it gave me a boost to work with all deliberation and speed to complete this book. It was during his Celebration of Life service that I understood the full impact of his statement. During his life span, he had filled many pages of the book of his own life, which his son, Romel, explained so dynamically and adequately, with lessons for everyone to remember. Perhaps, someone will write his book, "in absentia". Thank you, Deacon Paul! It was after Paul Showell's homegoing service that I also received the sub-title, **HE'S "GOTCHA" COVERED! Lenora R. Merritt-Showell!**

I must acknowledge all of those who have been such a wonderful blessing to me since the demise of my husband. You have allowed me to want for nothing. Those of you who have provided me with groceries, housecleaning, cooked meals and delivering them, phone calls and cards, flowers and chocolates, etc., etc., etc. Thank you from the bottom of my heart. Special appreciation and thanks to all my children and spouses, grandchildren and great grandchildren as well, who have helped me in any capacity. Thanks, love and blessings in abundance to you all.

Also, I want to acknowledge and dedicate this book of enlightenment to all future widows, particularly to everyone who reads, is encouraged, inspired, and helped by the revelations I received as I studied the rich word of God concerning widows. It is true that the Scriptures were written for our learning, our strengthening, our admonition, (correction) and encouragement.

One of the most influential individuals in my life concerning widowhood, among other things, was my own mother, Theresa Juanita Dyson-Merritt. She experienced widowhood for approximately 21 years prior to her transition. Although she lived alone about 10 of those years, before moving into a Christian owned and operated senior's residence. Through the years she shared many of her own experiences and encounters. Being the mother of sixteen children, (8 boys and 8 girls) it was prayer that sustained her. She was a praying woman!

I can recall an incident she told me about concerning a prayer time experience. My mother had framed a daily prayer time with the Lord. On a particular day she went upstairs to pray. She noticed the disheveled condition of the children's bedrooms and began to tidy things up. Suddenly, she said, when passing by one of the doors, it seemed to move without hands and struck her in the face. Immediately, she was reminded that she had come to pray and not to do housework. Of course, she said that she thanked the Holy Spirit for the reminder. She was not injured, but stopped everything and began to pray. That prayer seemed to have been the catalyst of sustaining grace for my oldest brother, who was in an accident on his job that very day. She so often told us that prayer is our pipeline to victory in any situation.

This occasion, which my mother shared, proved to be so

invaluable. Her testimony was about God's preservation, attention to details, and guardianship over her as her protector. My mother and a next door neighbor were close friends. They talked often about various subjects. One day Mrs. Johnson asked my mother how she had slept the night before. My mother's reply was, "Like a baby!" Well, Mrs. Johnson said, "I tossed and turned, and just could not get to sleep, so I decided to get up and sit by the open window. It was a warm night. There was an alcove between the two houses. Before long, up came a man and he began trying to break into the side entrance to your house. I couldn't believe my eyes. Then I said to the man, "If you can stand all these bullets from this gun, you just keep on trying to break into that house." Mrs. Merritt, she said, "I didn't have gun, the first. But that man ran like a bear was chasing him." You can just image how startling that news was to my mother. She thanked the neighbor for allowing the Lord to use her during that time of danger. Mrs. Johnson said that after that incident, she got back into the bed and "slept like a baby." They both had a big laugh about the experience. Does God care? All the time! Remember, God never slumbers and he never sleeps. He sees all you do and hears all you say. He'll be woke all night, so why not go to sleep?

There are many other stories and experiences in which God showed himself strong in the behalf of my mother. Our family, as large as it was, (18 in all) always had plenty of food to eat. In fact, there was always extra guest for dinner at the Merritt's house. Saturday was always "go to market day". My parents found favor with one of the merchants who owned a stall in the market and sold all sorts of fruits and vegetables. My parents were told to come to the market near closing time. Mrs. Irma (the merchant) gave over-stuffed and extra bags of food to them, saying that she would eventually have to discard the items which she had not sold. My parents were charged a very minimal amount or allowed credit until the following week, if necessary. We never knew what it meant to be hungry. Only eternity will be able to tell all the blessings they experienced. I believe that they are written in the book of the life of the **WIDOW** named, Theresa Juanita Dyson-Merritt.

Most of all, I acknowledge my late husband, Chief Apostle Aaron B. Claxton, without whom I would not be who I am today. He worked with and through the Spirit of the Living God to enlighten me concerning so many things. Actually, I believe we enlightened one another! Words cannot express how much this **WIDOW** has been, is being, and know I will be blessed in my life tremendously. I miss him so much! Thank you, Honey-Babe! Now, GOD is my daily companion, helper, protector, strength, guide, provider, lover and friend. I thank you, My Lord and Savior! YES!

My Maker is my HUSBAND! (Isa. 54:4)

Preface

It has now been almost three years since that unrealistic day for me, that Chief Apostle Aaron Bobby Claxton, my beloved husband, transitioned to glory. I think of him every day, many times a day, and re-live so many different occurrences. This is the month of December when I am writing this preface, and the unprecedented year, 2020 is coming to a close. I believe that this year shall live on in infamy for so many people. At last count, according to collected data, hundreds of thousands of people, worldwide have passed away due to the pandemic disease – Covid-19, and the count is increasing daily. So, death is everywhere, caused by a multiplicity of reasons, the world over. People need words of strength, hope, encouragement, and peace. May some of what is said in this book be a factor of fortitude and stimulate resilience (bounce back) in your spirit, mind, and body.

As I said above, I think about our husband/wife interaction and relationship every day: sometimes thoughts of joy, remembering the good times; sometimes thoughts of sadness, remembering that we no longer are experiencing things together; and sometimes there is a sense of loneliness without his presence. I can recall one day as I walked into the house, a blanket of grief seemed to have fallen over me. I wept loudly as I looked at his pictures on the wall. While gazing at him with tears running down, I heard the voice of the Lord ask me, "Why are you crying?" Since no one else was around, I said in a loud, mournful voice, "I am looking at him and I miss him." The Lord said, "Look at him again." I said, "I am looking at him, that's why I'm crying." I heard, "What do you see?" With another quick glance, I replied, "He's smiling in every picture." I heard, "Then, why are you crying?"

I have experienced the voice of the Lord often enough to know Him, so I knew who was speaking to me. When God speaks to me, maybe you too have experienced this, His voice comes to me, with an unexplainable peace which dries up my tears and calms my fears. I realized that God's questioning was not meant to say, stop crying. I sensed, on this occasion, that God wanted me to think about what I was thinking about, as I wept. It reminds me of Mary Madeline at the tomb of Jesus. She came there weeping bitterly, but left amazingly changed after her unanticipated encounter with the Lord (John 20: 15-18).

Not many days later, I began to understand God's inquiry and realized my fear. It was not just the absence of my husband's physical presence, the aching void in my heart, the sound of his voice now silenced, the wisdom of his words, or his smile that melted me at times, that I missed and which saddened me, as much as the thought that **widowhood** was now my legal identity. Widowhood was the primary "bugaboo" (a word from my childhood that my mother used often, meaning "underlying instigator") which also brought the tears and fears or fears and tears. It was something I had never experienced before and simply did not want to experience. I really felt ashamed to be called a widow. If the truth be spoken, for some reason, I associated my husband's death with a feeling of guilt; as if it was my responsibility to keep him alive; that somehow, I had failed in my obligation as his wife.

Then, I heard in my spirit, "Have you read my book about widows?" WOW! I hadn't even thought about that! And "Wow", you just keep on reading and you too, will discover that God always has every situation and circumstance covered before we get to it. He is just waiting for us to "dis-cover" it! Widows! God's got **you** covered!

After reading, mediating, and studying about widows in the bible, I decided to share what God had decreed about widows. For nothing is recorded in the bible by accident. Upon reading some biblical stories about widows, I decided to include strategic points learned from each of their stories. I call them "Points to Ponder". In addition, I have asked several other individuals who have experienced the stresses of Widowhood/Widowerhood if they would share an experience or two relating to some of their findings. They are recorded in the chapter entitled, "Heartfelt

Expressions". I am grateful to have had so many responses.

Perhaps you too will glean life-changing insights as you read and open your heart to hear from the Holy Spirit. I'm sure you will discover additional realities which describe your experience with widowhood.

ENJOY THE BOOK!

The Wonders of Widowhood
"God's Gotcha Covered!"

Introduction

It was a bright, but crisp Sunday morning, November 11, 2018, it was Veteran's Day. I was alone and other family members were attending our church. My eldest son, Bryan, now the Pastor of the New Creation Christian church, was carrying on in his usual manner. I made my way down the hall to my husband's hospital room where I had now been visiting for a week. As I was approaching the room, I met his primary nurse who informed me that her favorite patient had not responded to her as usual when she greeted him that morning. When I arrived in his room he turned his head toward me, eyes still closed, when he heard my voice. We greeted and exchanged thoughts. I noticed that his responses were mainly small gestures and low tones. I again kissed him and wiped away some tears from his eyes. Then, I decided to play some worship music and sat in a chair near his bed. After a while, I heard a strange sound which seemed to be coming from the bed. The attending nurse, who, no doubt, heard the same sound, came rushing into the room. "There was a strange noise coming from the bed, something like a whistling sound," I said. "I have no idea what it could be!" She responded with the fact that it was the release of air pressure coming from the bed, so she came to see what had happened. However, since everything looked and sounded the same as it did earlier, she left without further explanation, except that she wished that all the hospital rooms had such calming, delightful music in them. I noticed that the pumps and machines seemed to be still recording. The heart monitoring device looked the same and the noise from other machines were still audible. Yet, I felt something was different. I thought he was just sleeping. However, since the nurse didn't seem alarmed, I dismissed the apprehension. I waited a little while and attempted to speak to my husband again. There was no response, no motions, not even a groan this time. This elicited alarm! I hurried to the nurse's station to ask if the doctor would come and check on him.

Finally, two doctors came into the room and closed themselves in behind the curtain. It seemed to be quite a while before they came out. No words were spoken at first, but they shook their heads signaling his demise. They stood close by ready to support me. I fell into their arms and I felt numb. But LORD! We have prayed! We have fasted! I have quoted healing scriptures and posted them around the house! The family has set special prayer times to pray for his recovery! We have praised you for the victory! The church has prayed. We have not talked anything but healing and deliverance! What more could have been done?

I have learned to appreciate the way God operates in the Kingdom of God toward his kingdom citizens. It was when I became quiet and calmed my mind that He allowed me to hear and directed my attention to Hebrews 11, with specific focus on verse 39. "And all these, having obtained a good testimony through faith, did not receive the promise." That "WORD" has been a calming factor to me, through the Spirit!

Thinking back on what I heard that day coming from the bed, could that sound have been when his spirit took its flight from his body? I don't know! I was told, days later, that Apostle Bryan, while ministering that Sunday morning, suddenly stopped speaking. He then fell over the podium sobbing loudly. The congregation was in awe and silent before he regained his composure and continued with the message. He told me later that he heard the voice of his Dad bidding him farewell and encouraging him to bravely carry on the ministry. Several other individuals told me about their encounters during that same period of time.

When I left home that morning, I had no idea that would be the day God's General, in the Army of the Lord, the Warrior for Righteousness, my husband of 60 years, 5 months, and 10 days, 4 hours and 40 minutes, was to make his departure from earth to Glory. It was as if he had been waiting to speak to me that morning, and for us to greet one last time, on this side of glory. Little did I know that, at 2:20 p.m. on Veteran's Day, the 11th day of November, the 2nd Sunday of the month, in the year of our

Lord – two thousand eighteen, would mark the ending of one era and the beginning of a whole new season in my life called **"WIDOWHOOD."**

When I recall the months and days prior to the transition of my "Chief Apostle", I must admit that the goodness and mercy of the Lord has followed me throughout this whole ordeal. Time after time God had proven that his hand was upon me and that he was with me.

I remember especially, a month or two before, I was impressed by a tremendous testimony from Dr. Bill Hamon, presiding Bishop and prophetic voice of Christian International, Santa Rosa Beach, Florida, describing a victory he won in one of his warfare struggles. Prior to winning in his battle, he decided to dedicate himself to a month of prayer, praying in his heavenly language for an hour daily. He then challenged others to do the same when faced with seemingly insurmountable situations. I could not shake his testimony. The will to do that, just would not leave my mind. Although the responsibilities of being a "caregiver" for my husband was pressing heavily upon me, I decided to "just do it".

It seemed to be quite a press at first but I knew I needed the help of the Holy Spirit dwelling in me. I knew that I had the promise written in Jude, verse 20 which says; "But you, beloved, building yourself up on your most holy faith, praying in the Holy Spirit." I knew that I needed to be built up in mind, body and spirit.

I had also heard Dr. Bill Hamon talk about an experience that he and his wife had when they visited Hoover Dam in Nevada. The account is written in his book entitled, "Seventy Reasons for Speaking in Tongues". While watching, listening, and observing the Dam, the voice of the Lord began revealing revelatory insights to him concerning the operation of the power of the Holy Spirit in human vessels. Jesus said to his disciples; "But you shall receive power after that the Holy Spirit has come upon you . . ." (Acts 1:8)

Dr. Hamon wrote: *"The gift of a spirit language serves as one's own built-in hydro-electric power plant. The reservoir of water is dammed up and has a water-gate with a turbine in it. When the gate is opened, the rushing water causes the blades of the turbine to spin rapidly, which turns the big dynamos that produces electrical power to supply energy for several states. The reservoir is your spirit. One's water gate is the mouth; the Holy Spirit (water) resides within you, when speaking in tongues, the turbine, (the tongue), activates the spirit-dynamo to produce the powerful presence of God" to minister to your need.*

I sincerely believe that my obedience to the prompting of the Lord to pray in tongues for one hour every day for a month, was what I needed. It was manifested in the powerful presence of the peace of God which seemed to engulf me. It was that presence, which kept me from being so devastated during the weeks and months prior to and that followed the transitioning of my man of God, the man of my dreams, my dearly beloved husband. I am often asked how I was seemingly, so calm during the home-going service, that I could speak with such expressiveness and assurance before the listening audience. I asked myself the same question. I assure you that it was all God's peace and comfort, through the Spirit, and not me; especially, since it was not my decision to speak at all during that celebration service for Chief Apostle Aaron B. Claxton. My mind was settled on sitting quietly and allowing others to express themselves. I had no speech planned nor prepared. It was just prior to going into the service that one of the presiding bishops, Bishop James Nelson, asked me to have words to share. He spoke with such wise coercion, that there was no way out.

Looking back at that event I can only say in the language of the Apostle Paul, "That the life that I now live, I live by the strength of Christ Jesus who loved me and gave himself for me." How grateful I am for God's compassionate love, mercy and grace!

Even since that unexplainable experience, God has blessed me beyond measure. That is why I wanted to write this book to put in the hands of others who are experiencing, have experienced, and/or will experience the departure of their spouse or loved one. I am not saying that God will always use the same methodology for everyone that He used for me. But I do know, that God is well aware of what you are encountering, and truly cares about all those who rely on, trust in, and depend upon Him and His word. God does have a way that's mighty sweet, and He invites you to lay your burdens down at His feet!

**What He's done for me and others,
He will do for you!**

Chapter 1
THE WIDOW'S PLIGHT AND GOD'S MANDATE

Some definitions were taken from Merriam-Webster's Deluxe Dictionary:

Widow: An Old English word, akin to Old High German; Latin
- to separate from
- A woman who has lost her husband by death and usually has not remarried.

Widowhood: The state or fact of being a widow

Widower: A man who has lost his wife by death and has not remarried

Widowerhood: The period of time a man remains unmarried after losing his wife by death

Exodus 22:22–23
"You shall not mistreat any **WIDOW** or fatherless child. If you do mistreat them, and they cry out to me, I will surely hear their cry . . ."

Deuteronomy 10:18
"He executes justice for the fatherless and the **WIDOW**...giving him food and clothing."

Deuteronomy 24: 19
"When you reap your harvest in your field and forget a sheaf, you shall not go back to get it. It shall be for the sojourner, the fatherless, and **WIDOW**, that the Lord your God may bless you in all the work of your hands. When you beat your olive trees, do not go over it again, it shall be

for the...**WIDOW**. When you gather your grapes, you shall not strip it afterward. It shall be for the...**WIDOW**.'

Deuteronomy 27:19

"Cursed be anyone who perverts the justice due to the stranger, the fatherless, and the **WIDOW**." And all the people said, "AMEN!" (So, let it be! And, so be it!)

Isaiah 1:17

"Learn to do good, seek justice, correct oppression; bring justice to the fatherless, plead the **WIDOW's** cause."

Psalm 68:5

"Father to the fatherless and protector of **WIDOWS** is God in his habitation."

Psalm 146:9

"The Lord watches over the sojourners, he upholds the **WIDOW** and the fatherless..."

Jeremiah 22:3

"Thus said the Lord: Do justice and righteousness, and deliver from the hand of the oppressor him who has been robbed. And do no wrong or violence to the stranger, the fatherless, or the **WIDOW**, nor shed innocent blood in this place."

Proverbs 15:25

"The Lord tears down the house of the proud but maintains the **WIDOW's** boundaries."

Zechariah 7:10

"Do not oppress the **WIDOW** or the fatherless, the alien or the poor; and let none of you devise evil against his brother in your heart."

Malachi 3:5

"...I will draw near to you for judgement. I will be a swift witness against...those who swear falsely...against those who oppress...the **WIDOWS** and orphans, and do not fear me, says the Lord of hosts."

Isaiah 54:4

"Fear not, for thou shall not be ashamed, neither shall you be humiliated. You will not suffer shame and remember the reproach of your **WIDOWHOOD**. For your Maker is your husband – the Lord Almighty is his name – the Holy One of Israel is your Redeemer; he is called the God of all the earth."

James 1:27

"Religion that is pure and undefiled before God, the Father, is this: to visit orphans and **WIDOWS** in their affliction; and to keep oneself unstained from the world."

I Timothy 5:3–6 (NIV)

"Give proper recognition to those **WIDOWS** who are really in need. But if a **WIDOW** has children or grandchildren, these should learn first of all to put their religion into practice by caring for their own family, and so repaying their parents and grandparents, for this is pleasing to God. She who is a **WIDOW**, and left all alone, puts her hope on God and continues in supplication and prayers night and day. But the **WIDOW** who is self-indulgent is dead even while she lives."

I Timothy 5:9, 11, 14

"Let a **WIDOW** be counted if she is not less than sixty years of age, being the wife of one husband. As for the younger **WIDOWS**, when their sensual desires overcome their dedication to Christ, they want to marry. So I counsel younger **WIDOWS** to marry, to have children, to manage their homes and to give the enemy no opportunity for slander."

Chapter 2
THE WIDOW'S OFFERING

"May the Lord answer you in the day of trouble; May the name of the God of
Jacob defend you; May He send help from the sanctuary; May He remember
all your offerings . . . (Ps. 20: 1, 2)

We read in Mark 12:41-44 that Jesus sat down near the collection
box in the Temple and watched as the crowds dropped in their
money. Many rich people put in large amounts. Then a poor
WIDOW came and dropped in two very small copper coins, worth
only a fraction of a penny. Jesus called his disciples to him and
said, "I tell you the truth, this poor WIDOW has given more than
all the others who are making contributions. For they gave a tiny
part of their surplus, but she, poor as she is, has given everything
she had to live on." God evaluates your giving by what you have left
in your treasury after you have given. This widow passed the test of
sacrificial giving because she sowed all that she had. Now God is
obligated, according to his word, to see that she reaps an abundant
harvest. Our all does not defund God's all. Rather, it multiplies the
harvest that you reap.

God keeps a vigilant, even a watchful eye on the WIDOW. He
is very concerned about them. Psalm 68:5 speaks of his profound
disquieted Spirit that is aroused when anything and anyone seeks
to do them harm. God has clearly informed all created beings that
He is their provider, he's their protector, their fence and defense,
their guide, their supplier, their caregiver and their caretaker. The
Almighty, the True and Living One, is a true Father of widowed
daughters and sons.

God invites others to participate in the same attitude of giving
and being blessed accordingly. For with the same measure that is
given, with a cheerful attitude, and from a heart of gratitude, you
will be given in return. He is a father like none other! WIDOWS
are his heart and can pull on his heartstrings! SO, BE AWARE!

Most of all, God proclaims that He is a husband to the widow.
It was God who pronounced that "It is not good for "man"

(translated humankind) to be alone." He promised never to leave us (WIDOWS/WIDOWERS). Never to leave us alone! That is why He sent the Holy Spirit to dwell with us forever! Likewise, he sent his angels to protect and to encamp around us. Don't ignore Him! He's looking out for you!

POINTS TO PONDER:

1. This widow fulfilled one of God's principles for giving. She took no thought about what she would eat, drink, or put on, but gave all she had.
2. She was unaware that she was being observed by the One who owned everything and was her supplier.
3. Oh! That we would learn to trust the Lord as she did.
4. Her actions spoke volumes without her mouth uttering a word.
5. Only eternity knows how many, other than the disciples saw, and were impacted by her actions.

Chapter Three
THE THREE WIDOWS OF MOAB

"MANY are the plans in a men's heart,
But it is the Lord's purpose that prevails." (Proverbs 19:21)

I had never heard a story in the bible referred to as the three widows of Moab until I was sitting one day, meditating on the character Naomi, in the book of Ruth. The thought came so clearly, that Naomi was not the only widow in that story. There were three women who were widowed and each one has their own story to tell.

The historic setting of this story occurs during the period of the judges, but between the death of Joshua and the rise of Samuel's influence upon the Jewish nation. Specific commandments, laws, rules, and ordinances had been given to the nation of Israel by Moses, reinforced by Joshua, and established within Jewish households. This, of course, included instructions regarding interpersonal relational behavior within families where the head of households were concerned. This book reflects that aspect of family deportment.

At this juncture, I believe that it is worth noting that, heretofore, none of the titles of the canonized Books of the Bible contained the name of a woman. So, there necessarily must be something quite relevant and noteworthy about Ruth and her distinctiveness which netted her this sort of recognition.

The title of the Book of Ruth also indicates that she is a very significant character in this story; and she very well may be, depending upon which perspective or viewpoint is most pressing to the reader, at the time. Most commentaries highlight the Book of Ruth as a story that begins with a negative - famine, death and loss; but ends on a positive note - the sovereign grace and prevailing purpose of God. In addition, you will see an analogy between Boaz and Jesus Christ, our Kinsman-Redeemer.

Let me not fail to mention also that Ruth is in the Davidic, kingly genealogy of Jesus, the Christ, Son of the Living God. There are also other significant messages and lessons recorded in this book for our learning as well as for our admonition. You will discover as you read, what I learned in studying the story behind the story, which addressed my state of affairs termed "Widowhood".

The Book of Ruth opens with an explanation of a dilemma being experienced by a particular Jewish family dwelling in the land of Bethlehem, Judah. Perhaps, as migrant workers they lived off of the land. Since there had been no rain over a long period of time, the result was a devastating drought. This family consisted of the husband, Elimelech (meaning "My God is King"); his wife, Naomi – (delightful, pleasant, and lovely) and their two sons – Mahlon (Weak, Sickly) and Chilion (Failing, Pining). As priest of the family and cognizant of his responsibilities, Elimelech decided to move his family to a place where food was more plentiful. It was called the land of Moab. The Moabites were descendants of Lot, the nephew of Abraham. The Moabites disliked the Hebrews and had joined with Midian in battle and in cursing Israel for many years prior. (Num. 22:4) Nevertheless, Elimelech chose to dwell in Moab in an attempt to sustain his family.

The story doesn't tell how long the family had lived in Moab before Elimelech, Naomi's husband died. Now a widow with two sons, Naomi began to see her life on the decline. Shortly thereafter, her two sons chose Moabite women to marry. One wife was named Orpah (meaning "Fawn"). The other wife was named Ruth, which means (Friend- one born for adversity). Soon after the death of Elimelech, and not long after her two sons were marriage, the sons died also. It was said that the men in the family died while engaged in battle. I don't know. Now, there were three widows in one household. There was mourning, grief and sorrow, and unfulfilled hopes and dreams. This of course, added to the pains already being experienced. The three widows found themselves depending upon others for their wherewithal and daily sustenance.

Both daughters-in-law treated Naomi with the uttermost respect and kindness, assisting their Mother-in-law on every hand. It seemed that Naomi always received much support and attention, and suffered no want. Despite the loving care that Naomi received, there still must have been a nagging dissatisfaction with her status quo. According to Hebraic law the family of the deceased is released to go back home after ten years of living elsewhere. By then, Naomi must have reached her breaking-point. Furthermore, she heard that God had blessed her homeland and now there was an abundance of food. She talked with her daughters-in-law about going back to the land of her nativity. Obediently, they packed up their belongings and started on their way to Bethlehem. Perhaps, on the road back, Naomi recalled and talked extensively about many of her experiences in Bethlehem, as well as the laws and ordinances by which they lived. No doubt, the wives must had observed Elimelech and Naomi's rituals as they worshipped their God while in the land of Moab. There was excitement in Naomi's voice as they walked and she talked about her God and the miracles which he performed through the years. However, Naomi, in her wisdom, must have detected or discerned a quietness in the spirit of the two daughters-in-law. She realized that their experiences had not been like hers and that the idol god which they served and worshipped was not at all like her "True and Living God". Naomi stopped and encouraged the widows to return to their motherland. She blessed them saying, "The Lord deal kindly with you as you have dealt with the dead and with me. The Lord grant that you may find rest in the household of your husband." So they wept and kissed one another. But replied, "We want to go with you". Naomi affirmed again that they should return and find a husband among their own kin. It was as though Naomi wanted them to be persuaded in their own mind, whether to go forward or to go back home. Orpah acquiesced. Kissed Naomi again, wept and returned to her home.

There is a decision that every widow will eventually have to make when the loss of a loved one invades their life. There has been the severing of a bond made between the two of you and now you are left to venture into a new era or season of life broken, hurting, torn apart and alone. Others may suggest what to do next, pray and intercede for you, recommend, and/or make strong suggestions, but the final choice is yours to make.

As I continued to study this story about the three widows returning from Moab, there seemed to be a distinct representation being formulated concerning each of the widows. This is what I saw were the effects of widowhood upon each of them and how it affected their decision-making.

The stress and distress upon one of the widows caused her to become "paralyzed". To be paralyzed is to be frozen in time and activity. It is the inability to make new moves or changes as in previous times. The impact of her experiences of the past kept her living in the past. She seemed powerless to move beyond her own wounded heart. Perhaps, she had never learned that every human being is born with their own built-in purpose. And that her life was just as valuable to the Creator as that of her now deceased husband's life on earth. Her decision was to live in the past. Paralyzed by the hurt from the loss of her husband, and because she was accustomed to life as it had been, she made the choice to remain where she was. Although acknowledging the good and the blessings seen in the life of her mother-in-law, Orpah chose not go any further. She decided to go back to the familiar place of comfort, familiar people, familiar surroundings and habits. Sometimes events may cause individuals to feel as though they are not predestined to live differently or that they are not good enough for God's best. You may think that you are being punished (for whatever reason) because of the circumstances. Perish the thought!

Everything that has life will go through changes. Change in life is inevitable! Even in the face of apparent deliverance from the mundane, it is easier to remain with the familiar, or the comfortable path of life you're on, instead of moving beyond past experiences. Therefore, we chose to live within customary behavior patterns. Although tearful, Orpah was paralyzed by her present status and elected to go back to live in the past rather than to press forward toward a new and hopeful future.

Amazingly, another widow was "terrorized" by her present situation. Despite encouraging others, it is possible to feel terrorized momentarily by circumstances which seem beyond your control. Naomi had talked about the wonderful things that had happened in her life. She acknowledged the blessings which she had enjoyed throughout the years. She shared with others of the goodness and loving kindness of the God that she served. She had experienced favor and victory in life. Sometimes one may become so terrorized by their immediate situation that it blinds their mind. Naomi confessed that she had left her homeland full, successful, blessed and happy. She thanked those who had treated her with care and respect. But now, after the tragedies, all that loomed in her mind was the past negatives and the present heartfelt hurts, the losses, the deaths, as well as the lonely days and nights. Naomi even blamed God for her apparent dilemma. Actually, when her relatives, friends and neighbors commended her for what they saw as a progressive life, her reply was only an opposing one. "Don't call me Naomi," (delightful, pleasant, or lovely). "Call me MARA", (bitter) because The Almighty has made my life bitter. I went away full, but the Lord has brought me back empty. Why call me "Delightful, Pleasant or Lovely"? The Lord has afflicted me; the Almighty has brought misfortune upon me." She sounds like she had been terrorized. Why blame God for your negative images?

What a sad, debasing state to be in! Seeing and speaking only from a heart of grief and a selfish mind-set. Naomi was terrorized by her present situation, reacted bitterly, but I hope that she didn't live there very long. To be terrorized is to be frightened, threatened, and intimidated by how things appear at the present time. She was thinking only about herself and the changes which she now faced. The victories of the past, had not inspired Naomi to go forward. She had been so dependent upon the natural circumstances, that her grief did not allow her to see the presence of the supernatural. She must have forgotten about the goodness of the Lord in the land of the living. Naomi felt so terrorized by the present that she dared to step out and put her full confidence in the Almighty. What we learn from the past, will bring us to the present, in order to take us to the future! (Both negatively and positively)

Then, there was the widow, Ruth. She must have been a woman of insight, having the ability to learn from the past, while living in the present, and yet have hope and faith for the future. Naomi tried her utmost to convince her daughters-in-law to return from following her. Even after Orpah turned to go back, Naomi continued to test Ruth's determination to remain. Ruth replied, "Don't urge me to leave you or to turn back from you. Where you go, I will go and where you stay, I will stay. Your people will be my people and your God my God. Where you die I will die, and there I will be buried. May the Lord deal with me, be it ever so severely, if anything but death separates you and me." WOW! Naomi recognized sheer determination in Ruth's words and attitude, so she stopped urging her to go back.

There are occasions when a person cannot see in themselves what another individual can see emanating from their persona. Because of the testimony both lived and spoken by Naomi about her God, Ruth caught a vision for her future that Naomi could not and perhaps, did not see. Despite all and through it all, Ruth was "mobilized" by the words of Naomi to move beyond the past, realize the present, but look forward to the future. She decided to keep moving forward. Could it be that your testimony might be the catalyst which mobilizes someone else to move forward on their life's journey?

Ruth had a future and a hope and there was no denying it! She must have grasped something powerful about life and living that not even Naomi could see. She must have realized that Naomi had someone on her side with whom she wanted to develop a close bond and relationship. Nothing in Ruth's past could compare to what she imagined her future could be. It seemed as if Ruth was willing to submit to whatever was necessary to obtain that chance for a brighter future.

Ruth had no idea what God had already purposed for her future. As an apple, orange, watermelon seed has purpose in it, and it brings forth its potential when placed in the right environment, so Ruth was ripened in her new setting. Her future manifested her expectations and they began to unfold when she met and married Boaz. Hidden in the plan of God was Ruth's link to royalty and to the Messiah, Himself. For Boaz produced Obed by Ruth, Obed produced Jesse, and Jesse produced David, the King. Fourteen generations later, Jesus, the Christ was born. "And there shall come forth a rod out of the stem of Jesse, and a Branch shall grow out of his roots." (Isaiah 11:1, 10)

What about you, My Sister? YES! My Brother? Do not allow your temporary situation to rob you of your royal future. Did you realize that feelings are feelings; emotions are emotions; grief is grief; sadness is sadness; pain is pain; tears are tears; loneliness is loneliness, they are all gender neutral; whether displayed through a male or female body? I thought I would tuck that thought in at this point.

If you have been touched by the death of a loved one, how do you feel or see yourself? Have you been "Paralyzed" and feel that you cannot go any further in life without the active presence of the deceased one? Or "Terrorized" wanting to erase all the memories of the past because your life has taken a bend in the road unexpectedly? Or have you been "Mobilized" by the words and testimonies of others, or by the unction of the Spirit to move forward, even into unchartered waters, because you realize that the Almighty has you in the palm of His hand? Thank God for having brought you though the rough times and expect him to carry you into your blessed future. Ask Jacob about the blessing in the midst of the struggles. (Gen. 32: 22-32) Wake up! The morning has come. And there's much more that God wants to do through you and for you!

If the truth be known, at some point during your grieving period your reactions may resemble all three reactions. That is not to say, don't grieve, mourn, or weep. Nor is it to say that your heart doesn't feel torn apart, or that it doesn't hurt because of that individual's departure from your life. I can say, that if you are a true believer, you do not grieve as those who have no hope! Just don't get stuck in the negative too long or for the rest of your life! Don't blame God for what you don't see or understand at this point in time. Remember that we all have a departure date, whether by air or land. We know not the day nor the hour. Your spouse just left ahead of you. Should Jesus delay his coming long enough, your day is coming, too!

I find myself frequently, thanking God for having allowed me to have been such a vital part of and played such a key role in my husband's life. Sixty years is a long time to be united with one person. To have been chosen by God, who knows all things from the foundation of the world, for that purpose, is a blessing. I count it all joy to have shared in his calling and ministry; to know his strengths and weaknesses; to be a partaker in his pleasures and disappointments; and to be his confidant, his friend, his prayer partner and intercessor; the Daddy of our children. Yet, I know that life is not a "cut and dry" existence. But God, His word, His presence, His witnesses, His angels, and His comfort is ever present to console.

I say, as long as you are in the land of the living, "LIVE" until God's purpose and plan for your life is completed. I can now say sincerely, that everyone has a finish line. "Live" until you reach it! Then, you, like the Apostle Paul can say, "I've finished my course! I've kept the faith! I'm now ready...!" Remember, even Jesus said, when it was his time to depart, "It - Is - finished!" He then bowed his head and gave up the ghost! "No one takes my life," he said, "I lay it down!"

POINTS TO PONDER:

1. Every life has times and seasons.
2. Seasons come with sunshine and rain, stormy winds, and calm weather.
3. No season last forever, changes will come, prepare for them!
4. Your decisions often affect your future.
5. It pays not to make permanent decisions due to temporary circumstances.
6. Faith sees what you cannot see with your natural eyes.
7. Seize a God-given opportunity and walk through the door while it is open.
8. Sometimes what seems like a negative is a set-up for a positive.
9. Ruth had no idea that she was destined for royalty. How about You?

Chapter Four
THE WIDOW OF ZAREPHATH

"Instead of your shame you shall have double honor; and instead of confusion, they shall rejoice in their portion. Therefore in their land they shall possess double; and everlasting joy shall be theirs." (Isa. 61:7)

As we enter the Book of I Kings, chapter seventeen, we are introduced to a most notable, heretofore unknown, yet one of the most powerful prophets in the Old Testament. He dwelt in Tishbe, a city in Gilead, thus he was called a Tishbite, and his name was Elijah. No mention is made of Elijah's wife or family. He spent most of his time in the presence of the Holy God and traveled throughout the land of Israel. Elijah was an earthly mouthpiece for the Almighty One, who had given him a message of judgment to give to the reigning King of Israel, King Ahab. It was written that King Ahab did more evil in the sight of God than all the other Kings before him.

It is noteworthy to see that when judgement is poured-out as a consequence of sin, everyone, the just and the unjust, feel the brunt of its results. However, God will preserve, provide for and protect his anointed ones. The pronounced judgement given by Elijah, was, "there shall not be dew nor rain these years, except at my word." Just imagine what it would be like without rain for even three weeks! Water is the number one essential for sustaining all life on this planet. This judgement was in direct relationship to the sin committed by Israel, which was the worship of Baal as the "god of rain". Instead, Israel neglected to adhere to worshipping the "True and Living God," who supplies all of our need, according to his riches in glory.

When the brook by which Elijah resided and drank, also dried up because of the drought, the word of the Lord came to Elijah and instructed him where to go and what to do. "Arise, go to Zarephath," God said, "For I have commanded a widow to provide for you." When Elijah came to the gate of the city, indeed, there was a widow gathering sticks. Elijah asked her for some water and bread. Her reply was that she could get him some water, but the bread would be a problem. "You see", she told him, "I do not have bread, only a handful of flour in a bin, and a little oil in a jar. I am gathering a couple of sticks so that I may prepare a meal for myself and my son so that we may eat it and die." Flour in a bin and a little oil in a jar." That's all the resources that God needed her to provide, other than her willingness to obey. Give God what you have. He will do the rest! She did!! God did!! The blessings flowed from there!

Our God cares and protects his chosen ones. For where God guides, He provides; and where He leads, He feeds. Our God blesses going and coming! He sees everywhere and everyone. Miracles were not only given to Elijah because God had commanded the ravens to bring him bread and meat to eat; but God was setting a widow in place for multiple miracles. I believe that God softened the widow's heart to receive the words of the prophet. Even in the face of what seemed to be sure disaster, the widow followed the instructions of Elijah. It was also through the obedience of Elijah to go to a non-Jewish city; ask a widow for her last meal; and the widow complying with the request of God's prophet, the widow was blessed. Her son was blessed, and Elijah was blessed for many days, even for as long as the drought lasted. Later, God also threw in the restoration of the widow's son back to life, by the hands of the Prophet Elijah. Giving activates God's miraculous supply to flow back to the giver. Give and you shall receive!

Jesus said, "But I tell you truly, many widows were in Israel during the days of Elijah, when heaven was shut up for three years and six months, and there was a great famine throughout all the land; but to none of them was Elijah sent except to Zarephath, in the region of Sidon (Jezebel's idol-god worshipping homeland), to a woman who was a widow." (Luke 4: 25, 26)

Despite the fact that she was a Gentile by birth, this widow received miracle upon miracle because of her willingness to obey. Even in the face of foreboding pain, anguish, starvation and death, this poor widow was willing to hear the word of the Lord through the mouth of the prophet, Elijah. Therefore, her life and the life of her son was sustained for many days. A triple blessing was granted to her, her son, and to the man of God.   I beseech you to read the entire story in I Kings, chapter 17.

POINTS TO PONDER:

1. The brook dried up the same time the widow was running out of provisions.
2. Elijah and the widow were at the right place, at the right time, with the same need.
3. The widow's heart was receptive to the prophet's request, therefore she was rewarded.
4. Elijah's obedience to go to a Gentile woman, in a Gentile area, paid off with great dividends for both the widow, her son, and the prophet.
5. God is willing to bless the just as well as the unjust, who trust in his word.
6. There is always more instore for your obedience than you can ever imagine.
7. Not only did the widow and her son have provisions for the entirety of the drought, but Elijah ate, as well as, had a place provided for him to stay.
8. Those who bless widows are blessed in return.

Chapter Five
THE WIDOW OF NAIN

"But God demonstrates his love toward us,
In that while we are still sinners, Christ died for us." (Romans 5:8)

Here is another story in the bible about a widow. You will find it only mentioned in the book of Luke, the physician. After reading about this widow, who remains nameless, I realized a number of truths about the character of God revealed in this story. The 7th chapter of Luke records these unambiguous virtues in only seven verses – 11 thru 17. Learning about the character of God always allows us to see ourselves like we've never seem ourselves; despite the fact that we have been made in the image and likeness of our Creator. At times, when some heartfelt, even heart wrenching events and experiences seem to shake our faith, it's really designed to propel us forward in order to gain more knowledge of the Almighty and His "modus operandi" (that is to say, His methods of operating). Open your heart! Receive all that the Lord has for you, today!

Jesus, just the day before in Capernaum, had greatly commended a Gentile centurion for displaying extraordinary faith. He believed for, not only the healing of his servant, but most of all, he was commended for his understanding and response to an authoritatively spoken word. At first, the centurion sent Jewish messengers to Jesus, who pleaded and begged for him to come and heal the servant of this most prestigious centurion, saying that he loved their nation and had built them a synagogue. Jesus consented to go. However, when Jesus was not far away, the centurion sent a group of his friends with another message. "Lord," he said, "do not trouble yourself, for I am not worthy that you should enter under my roof. I did not even think myself worthy to come to you. But speak the word only, and my servant will be healed. For I am a man under authority, having soldiers under me. And I say to one, 'GO,' and he goes; and to another 'COME' and he comes. And to my

35

servant 'DO THIS' and he does it." Jesus marveled at such strong faith. It was in stark contrast to the kind of conviction displayed by the high ranking religious leaders in Israel, who quoted the law but often failed to live by it. Jesus considered the centurion's words to be, "commanding faith!" The centurion's servant was instantly healed.

Now the very next day, as Jesus was walking near a city called Nain, about a day's journey from his hometown, Capernaum, a massive crowd was following him. Then he saw another crowd of people coming out of the gates of that city. It was a funeral procession. A widow was weeping, along with other mourners, over the death of her only son. Remember now, she was a widow, which meant that she had already experienced the loss of her husband. When he knew what was happening, compassion gripped the heart of Jesus. Compassion is sympathetic consciousness of others' pain and distress accompanied by a strong, moving desire to alleviate it. Jesus was so touched by the feelings of her infirmities that he did not let the opportunity go by without relieving the pain, as only he can. Immediately, Jesus stopped the procession, laid hands on the coffin, raised the son from the dead, presented him to his mother, and changed the whole atmosphere and mind-set of all that were present. What an awesome Redeemer! The crowds must have been awestricken by such compassion.

POINTS TO PONDER:

1. The widow had not ask for the raising of her dead son. But Jesus did it anyway!

2. It was not the widow's faith nor the faith of the crowd with Jesus, nor the mourner which followed the widow, that elicited the miracle. But Jesus cared enough to act!

3. The widow and her son were no doubt, Gentiles, living in Nain. God so loved the world!

4. Jesus was touched with the feeling of her infirmities, her hurts and inadequacies! Compassion drew out the miracle power that was in Jesus!

5. Jesus' compassion did not stop at feeling sorrowful, but he was moved to use his power, his ability and his influence by the Spirit to alleviate the pain. He is not a selfish Savior!

6. I believe that on this occasion, the widow of Nain, received the overflow from the anointing of the previous miracle. Jesus, still energized by the Roman centurion's display of faith, blessed the widow too. It was an opportune time to increase the faith, deepen the love, heighten the compassion, and broaden the knowledge of the disciples. The outpouring was for the crowd that followed him, the crowd that followed the widow, and most of all, the believers in Christ today who read this account of what Jesus did. Aren't we all glad he did?

I have been so encouraged after learning, sensing, and experiencing the deep affection of God for me that I am exhilarated to reinvigorate the faith of others during their down times.

Chapter Six
MARY, THE MOTHER OF JESUS

"... Yes, a sword shall pierce through your own soul also,
that the thoughts of many hearts may be revealed." (Luke 2:35)

The prophet, Simeon, who lived in Jerusalem, and often visited the Temple during his lifetime, came there at the right time, on the right day, to see who he had long awaited to see. Luke records that Simeon was a just and devout man on whom the Holy Spirit was resident, who had been waiting for the "Consolation of Israel." It had been revealed to Simeon by the Holy Spirit that he would not see death before he saw the Messiah. Being prompted by the Spirit to go to the Temple at that time, Simeon saw Mary and Joseph bringing the child Jesus into the Temple. They were there to offer a sacrifice of "a pair of turtledoves or two young pigeons after Mary's 40 days of purification, which was to be offered, after the birth of a male child, according to the law. Simeon took the child up in his arms, blessed God, blessed the child, and blessed the parents. A prophetic word was given concerning the child as well as to Mary. It is interesting to note that nothing is recorded having been prophesied to Joseph. The words spoken were both pleasurable and unpleasant, satisfying and puzzling. Mary pondered all these things in her heart. Simeon said to Mary that her soul would be pierced through as though she had been pierced with a sword. What a word!

No doubt, the sword that pierced Mary's heart was manifold. Mary suffered cruel denigrations about her miraculously born son, the virgin birth! She heard chief religious leaders deride her son's life mission. She not only saw the death of her eldest child, but had experienced the death of her husband. On occasions, her own children would scoff at their brother's activities and adages. Death and derision is a painfully piercing sword! But, thanks be to God! For death has now lost the crushing, crucial sting it once had. Thanks to the sacrificial price paid by our Redeemer, Savior and Lord Jesus Christ!

Not often, when we think of Mary, the mother of Jesus, do we consider the fact that she had already suffered the death of her husband and was widowed by the time her eldest son died. By the time Jesus' ministry began at the age of 30, nothing seemed to be mentioned about Joseph, only alluded to in criticism or about his business of carpentry. Biblical scholars have concluded that Joseph, Mary's husband, had already passed off of the scene of time when Jesus began his earthly ministry. Jesus became obedient to his parents and went home with them after they had anxiously sought for him for three days, on their journey back to Nazareth from Jerusalem where family and friends had customarily attended the Feast of the Passover. We don't see Joseph, hear from him, and nothing is directly said about Mary's husband, Joseph, after the incident when Jesus was twelve years of age.

When Mary and Jesus, with his disciples went to the wedding feasts at Cana, Joseph was not mentioned. There was much merriment, eating and drinking with family members and friends. Where was Joseph? Mary advised Jesus concerning the necessity for more wine at the party, not Joseph! (John 2: 1-12)

When Jesus' mother and brothers, who seemed to be concerned about the mockery of their brother, came to speak with him as he was teaching a multitude of people, Joseph apparently was not with them. It seems that Mary was being supported by her other sons, even as the law required when the mother is widowed. Jesus had informed the family that he was to be about his Father's business. He was not speaking about Joseph, his father, but his heavenly Father. It was the business of restoring the Kingdom of God on the earth. (Matt. 12: 46- 50)

Certainly, as Jesus traveled from city to city, and the women ministered to his needs, at times Mary was a part of that group. Even during Jesus' mockery of a trial, Mary was also a part of those who stood by. When Jesus was on the cross, he was mindful of his widowed mother. His final words of acknowledgment to her was "Woman, behold your son!" And to the disciple whom Jesus loved – speaking to John – "Behold your mother." From that hour, Mary chose to accompany John to his home. Not with Joseph! A commentary says that, perhaps, Jesus preferred that John should shelter Mary because his brothers had not yet been "born again" as had John. Remember, there were times when Jesus' natural brothers belittled him, just as others had.

It was at least fifty days after Jesus ascended that we read about Mary, the widow, with other women, being assembled with the disciples in the upper room in Jerusalem. That's where we find Jesus' brothers with Peter and others as they chose someone to take the place of Judas, the one who betrayed Jesus. "These all continued with one accord in prayer and supplication, with the women, and Mary, the mother of Jesus, and with his brothers." (Acts 1:14) Perhaps by then, the brothers were convinced that Jesus really is "who he says he is."

POINTS to PONDER:

1. Mary was an appointed vessel of obedience to her earthy purpose.
2. God always prepares you for your planned purpose in life whether you realize it or not. It's up to you to choose or refuse it.
3. No individual is exempt from the price of pain, but God will, with it, give you his peace.
4. God will make way of escape, so that you can bare what comes your way.
5. Be sure to take HIS way, and lean not to your own understanding.
6. Stay under the spout where the blessings are pouring out.
7. There will always be others who can identify with the kind of pain you suffer and encourage you to go forward.
8. You are not alone unless you choose to be alone.
9. Make friends who will enhance your calling!

Chapter Seven
ANNA, THE EXCEPTIONAL WIDOW

"My steps have held to your paths; my feet have not slipped.
I call on you, O God, for you will answer me ..." (Ps. 17: 5, 6)

The widow, Anna, mentioned in just two verses in Luke 2:36-38, was a phenomenal woman. One of those women who had a remarkable purpose and mission in life, but who seemed to have operated in obscurity. However, Luke is careful to give her name; to inform everyone that she was the daughter of Phanuel, of the tribe of Asher; that she was a widow, that she lived in the Temple, and that she was a prophetess. All of which was very significant in the scheme of things, at that time in history. She was another person, like Simeon, who was at the right place, at the right time, who lived during the right generation, to meet the right people in order to fulfill her assigned mission.

The name "Anna" means "favor" or "grace." In Hebrew it means "to bend or stoop to kindness" and "to find favor and show favor." She was from the tribe of Asher, who was to "dip his foot in oil, and was to have shoes of iron and bronze" according to Deut. 33:24, 25. All of which was a prophetic sign of joy and happiness, as well as prosperity, and which denoted a special anointing for "strength of character".

Commentaries indicate that Anna seemed to have been in her twenties when her husband died. It was extremely unusual in that day (and ours as well) for a woman to be married for only seven years to her husband before his death and not choose to remarry. According to the Mosaic Law, the brother of the deceased was to marry his widow, if he chose to. Neither is it clear, in Luke's writing, whether Anna had any children. I think not, since she was a devout follower of the laws of Moses which established family obligations surrounding widowhood.

Luke does mention in his writings that Anna dedicated herself to prayer and fasting in the Temple. When Jesus was brought into the

43

Temple, Anna was present and was rewarded for her faithfulness. At eighty-four years old, she was still available to be used to fulfill her God-given mission in life. For at least sixty years of discipline and dedication, with prayer and fasting, she prophesied and witnessed to all those she met about the coming Messiah. She had to be fully persuaded that what she had been taught was truth. Now, it had all paid off!

Though just a babe, she saw him, she blessed the baby and his parents, and rejoiced to experience what she had long awaited. That is, to see the one about whom the prophets had spoken and about who she believed would come.

What an amazing widow!

POINTS TO PONDER:

1. Anna chose self-sacrifice over self-gratification.
2. Anna chose not to wallow in self-pity because of her circumstances.
3. Anna relied more on the words she received from her mentors then feelings.
4. Anna was faithful despite the prolonged years of self-denial.
5. Opinions of others did not deter her determination. She didn't give up.
6. The blessings of faithfulness far outweigh temporary pleasure.
7. Age is not a factor when God wants to use your availability.

Chapter Eight
THE PERSISTENT WIDOW
Luke 18: 1-8 (AMP)

I found this parable to be one of the most fascinating, informative and insightful parables of all that Jesus used in discussing the Kingdom of God as it relates to widowhood. I chose the Amplified version of the bible for more clarity of understanding.

"Now Jesus was telling the disciples a parable to make the point that at all times they ought to pray and not give up and lose heart, saying, 'In a certain city there was a judge who did not fear God and had no respect for man. There was a [desperate] widow in that city and she kept coming to him and saying, 'Give me justice and legal protection from my adversary'.

For a time he would not; but later he said to himself, 'Even though I do not fear God nor respect man, yet because this widow continues to bother me, I will give her justice and legal protection; otherwise by continually coming she [will be an intolerable annoyance and she] will wear me out."

Then the Lord said, "Listen to what the unjust judge says! And will not [our just] God defend and avenge His elect [His chosen ones] who cry out to Him day and night? Will He delay [in providing justice] on their behalf? I tell you that He will defend and avenge them quickly.

However, when the Son of Man comes, will He find [this kind of persistent] faith on the earth?"

A parable is a natural depiction of a spiritual truth that may compare or contrast one actuality with the other. Most parables used by Jesus were similes (showing "like" or "as". This parable demonstrates a contrasting picture between God's kingdom affairs and the kingdom of men. The Lord asked his disciples if they were listening and really understood to what the unjust judge was eluding. Jesus elucidated on the difference between the "Just Judge" who will speedily defend and avenge his chosen ones (widows), and an unjust judge who had no regard for widows, nor concern for anyone but himself; no, not even the Creator of all mankind. What a contrasting picture between the Kingdom of Heaven and the kingdom of men!

"However, [in some Bibles the word used after the Lord's first point is 'nevertheless'], which means, 'despite the facts mentioned before', there is a higher truth which is vital and noteworthy. This widow demonstrated the kind of [undeniably persistent] faith in response to her prayer petition which He expects to see in all of his Kingdom citizens, upon his return to the earth.

POINTS TO PONDER:

► The affairs in the kingdom of men should resemble the affairs in the Kingdom of God if indeed we pray that 'God's kingdom come on earth as it is in Heaven'.

► Jesus was quick to point out any mistreatment of widows by others, especially those in authority, because they should know the laws of God.

► Although God is a defender and protector of widows, the added virtue of persistence for our rights as Kingdom citizens, wins the battle every time.

► This widow demonstrated the knowledge of her right by law, and got it.

► Her persistence, determination, and tenacity demonstrated her faith.

► Persistence pays off in the "long run" or the "short run".

► God is searching for those who will persevere in faith.

► Let's not forget the lesson learned here and follow suite.

Elisha, a protégé of Elijah, while on a ministry tour, met a certain woman who had been married to one of the sons of the prophets. She cried out to Elisha saying, "Your servant, my husband is dead, and you know that your servant feared the Lord. And the creditor is coming to take my two sons to be his slaves." So Elisha said to her, "What shall I do for you? Tell me, what do you have in your house?" And she said, "Your maidservant has nothing in the house but a jar of oil." Then Elisha said, "Go borrow vessels from everywhere, from your neighbors – empty vessels, do not gather just a few."

The widow was obedient to do all that Elisha said. He admonished her to go borrow as many containers as could be found, (possibly large and small) to go back home, shut the door behind her and her sons, and then pour the oil into all those vessels. They were to set each vessel aside as they were filled up. The unnamed widow followed Elisha's directions to the letter. The size of the jar from which she poured the oil was not mentioned in the text. However, when she was pouring oil out of the jar, and there were no more vessels which her sons were handing to her, the oil ceased. She went back to the man of God to report what had happened. He then gave her further instructions concerning what to do. Elisha told her to go, sell the oil that was poured out and pay her debt; and that she and her sons were to live on the rest of the proceeds. This was no doubt, the biggest miracle the family had ever seem. What a memorable experience for her and her sons to witness and to play a major part in!

I recognize the resemblance in the performance of this miracle and the miracle performed by Elisha's mentor, Elijah, in the reproduction of oil. History declares that Elisha doubled the number of miracles done by Elijah. In both cases, a widow was the beneficiary.

What is this story communicating to us about the wonders of God's provision for and concern on the behalf of widows? I found these insightful take-away lessons from this story:

POINTS TO PONDER:

1. The widow did not wait for the man of God to come to her, but she found him. Sometimes, God waits for us to trust in his unfailing love when we are distressed about problems.
2. She must have known of the Prophet's position and status with God through her husband's relationship, training, and teachings from the prophet. It was of benefit to the family not just to her husband.
3. Her husband's fear of God put the family in good standing (favor) with the prophet and God.
4. Never forget that crisis situations always present opportunities for miracles, creativity, new adventure, and manifestations of blessings.
5. Obedience is better than sacrifice, and that pride always goes before destruction and failure.
6. Blessings were never meant only for the individual who is in a crises state of affairs, but it will benefit others around you.
7. The widow used the Kingdom keys to unlocked her victory: (Luke 11: 9,10)

> Call unto me and I will answer;
> Ask of me and it shall be given;
> Seek my face and I will be found;
> Knock it shall be opened to you!

Chapter Ten
THE EARLY CHURCH WIDOWS

The Book of the Acts of the Apostles records the establishment of "the church", as it was referred to, after the ascension of Jesus, the Christ; who was also called "the Messiah"; "the Promised One" or the "King of the Jews". Jesus' purpose for coming to earth was not to establish a religion but to restore the order of Kingdom dominion to the legal inhabitants of the earth. The Book of Acts records the spread of what was called "Christianity," from its beginnings in Jerusalem to Rome, following Jesus' commission to "make disciples of all nations." It also tracks the step-by-step expansion of its beliefs and practices; its problems and solutions. Widespread persecution broke out and believers were scattered westward from Palestine to Italy, sowing the seed of the gospel as they went. Church policy was instituted and principles established to maintain order among the people. Since the gospel of the kingdom of God was first preached to the Jews, many Jews sought to adhere to their customs and practiced in the New Testament Church.

The gist of the laws, ordinances, and commandments given by God in Old Testament scripture, hold hidden truths even in the formation of the New Testament church. It is a fact that the Old Testament is the New Testament concealed; while the New Testament is the Old Testament revealed. Jesus spoke plainly to the religious leadership during his day, that he did not come to destroy the law, but that the law might be fulfilled. (Matt. 5:17) Thus, you find that as the church in Jerusalem was inaugurated, provisions were also made for widows. Chapter one in this book gives a lists of edicts pertaining to widows written in the Old Testament.

Mark 12: 42 makes mention of the poor widow who, when she entered the place of worship, brought an offering. It was all she had, and willingly sacrificed the equivalent of one eighth of a cent as an offering. Secretly observing, Jesus applauded her giving and proclaimed to his disciples that she had given more than the rich people. She gave out of her poverty, they pinched out of their riches, and had so much more left over to give, but didn't. God looks on the heart, while humans look mainly from an outward or physically visible appearance.

Paul speaks on this wise in his letter to Timothy, the Pastor of the church, about honoring and conducting business regarding the widows attending his church, in I Timothy 5: 1- 8 (MSG) He writes:

"Don't be harsh or impatient with an older man. Talk to him as you would your own father, and to the younger men as your brother. Reverently honor an older woman as you would your mother, and the younger women as sisters. Take care of widows who are destitute. If a widow has family members to take care of her, let them learn that religion begins at their own doorstep and that they should pay back with gratitude some of what they have received. This pleases God immensely. You can tell a legitimate widow, the way she puts all her hope in God, praying to him constantly for the needs of others as well as her own. But a widow who exploits people's emotions and pocketbooks – well, there's nothing to her. Tell these things to the people so that they will do the right thing in their extended family. Anyone who neglects to care for family members in need repudiated the faith. That's worse than refusing to believe in the first place."

Paul adds more instructions to Pastor Timothy in verses 9 – 16 of the same chapter:

"Sign some widows up for the special ministry of offering assistance. They will in turn receive support from the church. They must be over sixty, married only once, and have a reputation for helping out with children, strangers, tired Christians, the hurt and troubled. Don't put young widows on this list. No sooner will they get on, then they'll want to get off, obsessed with wanting to get a husband rather than serving Christ in this way. By breaking their word, they're liable to go from bad to worse, frittering away days on empty talk, gossip, and trivialities. No, I'd rather the young widows go ahead and get married in the first place, have children, manage their homes, and not give critics any foothold for finding fault. Some of them have already left and gone after Satan. Any Christian woman who has widows in her family is responsible for them. They shouldn't be dumped on the church. The church has its hands full already with widows who need help."

Let's see what happened in the church as it grew and included some of the Gentile congregants.

(Acts 6: 1-7 MSG)

"During this time, as the disciples were increasing in numbers by leaps and bounds, hard feelings developed among the Greek-speaking believers – "Hellenists" – toward the Hebrew- speaking believers because their widows were being discriminated against in the daily food lines. So the Twelve called a meeting of the disciples. They said, "It wouldn't be right for us to abandon our responsibilities for preaching and teaching the Word of God to help with the care of the poor widows. So, friends, choose seven men from among you whom everyone trusts, men full of the Holy Spirit and good sense; we'll assign them this task. Meanwhile, we'll stick to our assigned tasks of prayer and speaking God's Word. The congregation thought this was a great idea." And might I add, "A God idea." They went ahead and chose seven individuals. "Then, they presented them to the Apostles. Praying, the apostles laid hands on them and commissioned them for the task. The Word of God prospered. The number of disciples in Jerusalem increased dramatically. Not least, a great many priests submitted themselves to the faith."

Our God is a God of order. He not only set the world in order, but demands that the work of the ministry, which is done in His name, (represents Him) be organized and orderly operated.

Look at the results of peace, prosperity, harmony and unity:

"Behold, how good and how pleasant it is for brethren (and sisters) to dwell together in unity, (says Ps. 133:1, 3) For there the Lord commanded the blessing, even life for evermore."

"The blessing of the Lord, it maketh rich, and he addeth no sorrow with it." (Prov. 10:22)

Chapter Eleven
HEARTFELT EXPRESSIONS!!

Heartfelt Expressions is the chapter specifically set aside to allow other widows and widowers to share some of the experiences, feelings, pain and sorrow endured due to the passing of a spouse. They also share stages of mood swings, mindsets, and emotions encountered throughout their times of "bouncing back."

I mentioned in an earlier chapter that grief is not germane to a specific gender. Whether male or female, the effects of grief can be experienced by anyone. The manifestations of grief may vary from person to person, and/or from male to female. Likewise, siblings experiencing the death of a parent may react differently. The manifestation of that deep distress may take on various negative behavior patterns, even years later. Death shatters the very core of one of life's greatest human needs, and that is, a sense of security.

I trust that you will allow what is communicated help you through your time of grief. That it will also enable you to realize that you are not alone in what you are experiencing. Most of all, that you may grasp the Spirit of hope in God, who is eternal. I hope you will understand that there is a purpose for your life, thereby causing you to endure through the pain to complete your purpose. And that you may grasp the peace in knowing that God truly cares for you. He knows who you are. He even knows your name, where you live, and what you are going through. You will than, because of your faith and trust in God, comprehend that He is a friend that sticks closer than a brother; one who will never leave you nor forsake you; and that He loves you more than words can express.

1. Here is what Janice R. had to say after the transition of her husband William:

At the time of Bill's transition, we had been married for about 25 years. We had developed a close relationship for 9 years prior to our marriage. We met in our workplace.

My most unforgettable experience after Bill's passing was coming home a week after the funeral and realizing how quiet the house was. I tried to make myself feel "normal" by telling myself that Bill was in a better place, no longer in pain or suffering, as he had been over a year. Then, total sadness took over, because I had lost my best friend. A best friend that I relied on to help make the major decisions in my life; a best friend who was my teacher, my hero, and my prayer partner.

How do you pick up the pieces? Then, I reflected on conversations that Bill and I had. He always told me that, through Christ, I was strong and had healing hands, and my mission was to bring "peace and joy" to others. I felt that these words were coming from God through Bill because when I thought of these words, I certainly would feel "peace and joy" come over me. I thought about how Bill was never afraid of "death", and I began to feel a sense of relief that Bill was OK.

I have found that living as a widow is sort of a "transition" for me. I feel blessed that Bill was a true man of God. I know that Bill is no longer in his body, but reflections from him live on in me. I often recall him saying to me, whenever I get anxious or fearful, "take your troubles to God, and then let Him handle them, and keep your eyes and ears open to follow his lead."

Through this season of Covid-19, I have had plenty of time to pray and meditate throughout the day and I have found "peace and joy", just like Bill said I would.

Thank you Sister Janice!

2. Let's hear from Karen A. after the transition of her husband, Cleavon. She refers to it as: "The Valley of the Shadow of Death"

As I walked through the valley of the shadow of death, I found hidden treasures of darkness and grace like I never knew before.

I found God to be my strength in weakness. I became a widow in 1997, at the age of 37. My husband, Cleavon, suddenly transitioned at the young age of 39. I then found myself suddenly in a strange land, with a gaping hole in my heart and the daunting responsibility of raising three sons.

Cleavon and I met when I was a senior in college, after a gap year to have and nurture my then, one-year-old son. We met through family and mutual friends. Many things drew me to him. He had a smile and warmth that lit the room and an infectious laughter that endeared him to many. I was most impressed with his instinct to love and protect my son and myself. We were married for thirteen foundational and formative years of our lives, during which time we were blessed with two additional sons. Cleavon became my supporter, sounding board, chief cheerleader and my balance in supporting the work of God, even though he himself was not involved in ministry. I became the "sanctifying" wife that led to his salvation, before he went to meet our heavenly Father. I thank God for his reassurance, when I most needed it, that none of His good promises concerning my husband fell to the ground.

God has proven Himself true to His promise to never leave or forsake us. I gained an appreciation of the 'village' of family, church family and friends, as God used many to fill the voids and help to meet needs in the lives of my sons and myself.

The deep despair and grief that I found myself in at that time, allowed me to know God in a new way, as the God of all comfort and my keeper. The God who has now empowered me to aid in the comfort of others. I found worship to be a place of healing, transparency, and sweet fellowship with my healer. The most important nugget that I would share with others is to allow yourself the permission to grieve. Take the time and receive the grace to feel, to process, and to heal.

God has now allowed me to love again and to marry an awesome 'Man of God' who gives me love, covering and space to further process and feel, as needed, the scar that yet remains. I'm grateful for this new chapter which is not mutually exclusive from my previous chapter, and yet not diminishing nor dismissive of the love, the loss, and the lessons learned in my season of grief. GLORY BE TO THE NAME OF OUR GOD!

Thank you Sister Karen!

3. Lenora S. shares the Lord's sustaining grace, during the three months after her husband, Paul transitioned.

I married Paul when we were in our early twenties, 1966 to be exact. In my younger years, I thought I couldn't stand him because he used to tease me all the time. I later found out that he was shy and was trying to make an impression on me. Well, he did and the rest is history! (Maybe "our-story") When he was drafted during the Vietnam War, before leaving we promised to look at the North Star each night that it was shining, so we would always be connected. YES, I KNOW THE TIME ZONE WAS DIFFERENT! We were young and in love.

We were married for more than 55 years when Paul passed. As I write this, it's been less than 3 months since he transitioned on March 18, 2021, and the impact of his death is still emotionally fresh. Psalm 146:8-9 has strengthened me while working through this process of recovery.

"The Lord opens the eyes of the blind: The Lord raises them who are bowed down; The Lord loves the righteous; The Lord watches over the strangers; He relieves the fatherless and widows; but the way of the wicked He turns upside down."

It is the Lord who keeps me standing while feeling cast down. He CARRIES me as I walk while holding His hand. As you go through your time of adjustment, just remember …"He sustains the fatherless and the widow."

Lenora also included this reading from Henry Ward Beecher:

"When the sun finally drops below the horizon in the early evening, evidence of its work remains for some time. The skies continue to glow for a full hour after its departure. In the same way, when a great or a good person's life comes to its final sunset, the skies of this world are illuminated until long after he is out of view. Such a person does not die from this world, for when he departs, he leaves much of himself behind – and being dead, he still speaks."

Thank you Elder Lenora S.

4. Pastor Samuel B. shares a widower's wisdom and experiences related to times of grief and pain due to the transition of his wife, Sister Geraldine B.

To those who are reading this chapter, I want to convey this message, especially to the men. It is Okay to cry when you lose a spouse or a loved one. So many men today have been conditioned by society and a macho spirit not to cry. I recently lost my dear wife of 38 years to lung cancer. It has been only three months since she passed away, that I was asked to share this with the readers. My wife and I met at our workplace – Social Security Administration – ages 31 and 33. There is not one day that has gone by that I have not shed tears in the loss of my wife, who was a great woman of God. My most unforgettable experience after my wife's transition was how the Lord let the sunlight of His love pour through her room at the hospital. It had been a cloudy, gray day. That was an amazing sight to see!

Men! God is the one who gave us tears to help with the healing process. The tears that we shed are not shed in vain. God knows of every tear that we shed in our loss while mourning and grieving. Psalm 56:8 (GW) records: *"You have kept a record of my wanderings. Put my tears in your bottle. They are already in your book."*

Dr. Karl Menninger states, and I quote, "Weeping is perhaps the most human and universal of all relief measures."

A study done at the University of Minnesota by researchers found that there is a difference between emotional tears and tears shed as a result of wind or from the cutting of an onion. Emotional tears seem to contain two important chemicals related to one of the body's natural pain-relieving substances. Tears, they tell us, have an exocrine substance, like sweat or exhaled air. One of the functions of this processes is to cleanse the body of substances that accumulate under stress.

I have had to come to grips now with the fact that my wife is no longer around me. She was my constant companion and now she is gone. All I have is the memories as I cried out in my anguish and despair to the Lord, on more than one occasion this past week, just like blind Bartimaeus did.

So, men go ahead and cry. Do not try to hold your tears back! As you do you will get a release from all the pent up emotions inside of you!

Thank you, Pastor Samuel B.

5. A message from Doris K. and her valued relationship with Burdell K.

I honor my husband and I value our relationship. I am grateful for the many delightful memories he provided me with for 39 years. I thought our union could not be better. I thought it was heaven ordained and that it completed me. My husband passed away at age 83 from lung cancer. He had always tried to allay my fears concerning natural life situations and was ever ready with sustenance for me in every area. His passing rocked my world.

I called to mind that my parents had talked about God to my siblings and me as young kids. There was a time that I KNEW OF God, but I DID NOT KNOW God. I had no personal knowledge of God. I had no personal relationship with God. I was thrust into an all-out search for Him. But now, Praise God, I have been drawn into His Kingdom by His Holy Spirit. Unbeknownst to me, I thought at the time, I was the pursuer of God. In retrospect, I can plainly see, God was the pursuer of me.

During the process of reflecting on widowhood, I am inspired to approach it from this unique perspective. At our union, my husband made me his bride. In his death he made me his widow. Now, more importantly, I have become a bride eternally through Jesus Christ. My status will never be altered. I am His Bride for all eternity. I am His beloved and He is my beloved. What a glorious permanent union and relationship. The life I now live is by His faith and in His word.

Because life must go on for me, these are His words that I have learned to live by:

- ► He loves me with an everlasting love (Jer. 31:3a)
- ► He is the author and finisher of our relationship. (Heb. 12:2a)
- ► He draws me with His loving kindness. (Jer. 31:3a)
- ► He gives me hidden treasures of darkness and hidden riches of secret places. (Isa. 45:3)
- ► He clothes me in His righteousness. (I Cor. 1:30)
- ► Every promise He makes to me in Him is yea and amen. (2 Cor. 1:20)
- ► He is mine, I am His.
- ► He keeps me as the apple of His eye. (Ps. 17:8)
- ► His love is better than wine. (Song of Sol. 1:2b)
- ► He hides me under the shadow of His wings. (Ps. 91:1)
- ► He is my lover. He bids me, arise and come away with me. (Song of Sol. 2:13)
- ► He promises never to leave me nor forsake me (Heb. 13:5c). I found He will use whosoever and or whatever to draw one to Himself. There, one can experience His ever-present presence. Today, I have my own personal relationship with Jesus Christ. He continues to lavish me with the joy of experiencing His eternal love. His joy is the strength of this "erstwhile" widow.

Thank you Sister Doris!

6. "A Widower's Lament" was written by Deacon Samuel R. M. Sr. subsequent to his wife Yvonne's transition in death.

Many people say, "I know how you feel, because I lost a loved one also". Do you really know how I feel? Yes! I know what was meant. Whether because of an accident, illness, murder, or even war, the lost is painful. In my situation, my wife, of forty years, died from stage four breast cancer. On one hand, it seemed to have happened over night. Yet in retrospect, there was evidence of changes occurring but not identifiable with that specific illness. This was just the start of my inquiring mind. "What did I do to cause this situation to happen?" "Was I angry with her and said something that I really didn't mean?" "Did I really get a chance to say good-bye?"

For several months, prior to her death, I encountered one frustrating event after another involving several hospitals, two nursing homes, getting a biopsy, Chemotherapy, having a blood transfusion, and physical therapy. Would you believe that I spent an entire day searching for my wife, after being told that she was taken from the nursing home by ambulance to a designated hospital, only to find that she was not there? After calling several hospitals to no avail, I called my children and asked them to help me to find their mother. For me, there was actually, an exhausting final few weeks of her life. The events are too numerous and complicated to discuss.

Over the course of time, my wife's whole personality began to change. She was easily frustrated, and often demonstrated negative aggressive behavior. What appeared worst of all was that she seemed to have lost all love for me. Just a few months before her final days and weeks of life, we had celebrated our 40th wedding anniversary and she was in her right mind. I felt so guilty that I let this happen to my wife. I prayed to God to let her be healed and healthy. Let her be happily married to me again, and I would do what he wanted me to do. I would even do as Jesus did and call her back to life, if she died. Shortly after that, she suffered a stroke and was rushed back to the hospital for the last time.

It has now been more than 15 years since that time. As I look back at things, I see God directing my steps in the right direction. I decided to complete my degree in Economics and Psychology. The course in Psychology dealt with death and unpleasant experiences. This was the beginning of a divine healing process. We discussed the Five Stages of Grief:

1. <u>Anger</u> – I was angry with the doctors, the medicine, the Caregivers, and myself.
2. <u>Denial</u> – I denied that I would let her die. I would be Jesus and heal her. But I did not.
3. <u>Bargaining</u> – I prayed to God that I would do whatever He wanted if she could live.
4. <u>Depression</u> – I looked at wasted and unfulfilled dreams of retirement with my wife, no new career job or business; I saw nothing but loneness and isolation for myself.
5. <u>Acceptance</u> – Have I really accepted her absence? Sometimes I still feel guilty, thinking it was all my fault because I wanted some "alone time". Now, I have all the alone time I can use! I am learning, little by little. Thank you God for your presence, and your loving care!

Thank you, Deacon Merritt

Chapter Twelve
A PRAYER FOR WIDOWS/WIDOWERS

Father, in the name of your only begotten son, Jesus, I come boldly to the throne of grace in behalf of Widows/Widowers. The grieving, and the lonely. Forgive us for our transgressions and our debts, even as we forgive our debtors and those who have transgressed against us. I thank you now, for forgiveness.

I come before your presence with thanksgiving, knowing that there is no God like you. None and nothing can be compared to you. I enter your gates with thanksgiving because of the marvelous things which you have done in my life. I know that your promises are "Yea" and "Amen" in Christ Jesus. How grateful I am that you are mindful of us, our children, our affairs, and our well-being. O God, those who seek our harm will have to answer to you when we call upon your name.

Father, I come into your courts with praise because of who you are. I know that from everlasting to everlasting, you are God. Your word never changes. Heaven and earth may pass away, but you, my God, are the eternal one. Your word instructs us to look unto you, for you are our Creator, our provider, our door-opener, our way-maker, our friend that sticks closer than a brother. What times I am afraid, I will trust in you. What times I feel lonely, I know that you will never leave me nor forsake me. What times we long for our loved ones, who have departed, to yet be by our side, you know that all too well. For you can be touched by the feelings of our infirmities. Thank you for allowing me to spent the times, the seasons, and the years with my loved one, here on earth. It was not time wasted. I know that your eyes see and behold all things. I know that your ears are open to my cries. I know that no weapon formed against me prospers. And that every tongue that rises against me in judgement, I have authority to condemn it. I condemn every negative thought.

Almighty and all wise God, as I traverse this era, this phase, and this chapter in my life, I know that you are with me. Your rod of correction and your staff that guides us is ever present to lead us in green pastures and beside still waters. You prepare a table before us, even in the presence of our enemies. You anoint my head with oil. My cup of joy, peace, love, grace and mercy is running over. Now, even in these times of bereavement. My God, you are the strength of my life. Strength like no other! Help like no other! Grace like no other! Wisdom like no other! Thank you, my Lord and Savior, for you are my Lover and friend. I give you all the Praise, the Glory and the Honor, in Jesus name and for his sake.

AMEN! AMEN! AMEN!

Chapter Thirteen
CONCLUDING THOUGHTS

The writings in this book entitled, THE WONDERS OF WIDOWHOOD, began with a prompting within me, under the inspiration of the Holy Spirit, as well as encouragement, prodding, and biddings by several acquaintances. Little did I realize the wealth of information, insight, and strength I would acquire by the time I completed this book. My hope and desire is that all who read its contents will likewise receive from its pages some measure of relief, peace, comfort, and resilience during their time of grief, pain and sorrow.

Tears of grief continue to spring up within me, both visibly and invisibly, when I think of millions of individuals who claim that they want nothing to do with the God of the Bible. They do not seem to understand that their very existence is because of the sustaining grace, abundant mercy, unfailing love, unequaled wisdom, and the bounding omnipotence of the one True and Living God. He is the God of all creation and by Him all things exists. God made EVERY THING out of NO THING!

David, in Psalm 8, extols the greatest which characterizes God because of the unique significance and value of human beings to our Father God. Humans are the pinnacle of His creation, everyone is precious in His sight and the object of his watchful care. I don't think it is more evident than what is shown in His directive concerning widows.

Throughout the Old Testament, as well as some fulfillment in the New Testament, strict attention is given to widows. At least eight to ten demonstrations are given or mentioned in the Bible which emphasizes the significance of the widow. I attempted to identify lessons drawn from a variety of specific occasions where precautions were given because of the status of widowhood. Esteem and recognition was specified even in the New Testament churches. Few churches today seem to maintain that recognition of widowhood as was the mandate at the beginning of the Church. Nevertheless, God has not changed his mandate and I am living proof of that fact.

The very first encounter that I had after my husband's transition, was a test of my trust and faith in God as my "door-opener." The family was celebrating my granddaughter, Erryn's 25th birthday at a downtown restaurant. Of course, street parking was very limited so I decided to use a parking facility close by. The door was opened so I drove in and found a convenient place to park. I saw no one, but had already gotten a ticket upon entrance, and walked to the restaurant. We enjoyed the food, the fellowship, the games and conversations, as well as the gift-giving. When it was over, my daughter, Michelle, volunteered to drive me back to the parking garage. When we got there, everything was shut up tight and no one was in sight. I went from one end to the other side of the building. I tried every door I saw. Finally, I noticed a sign on the building saying, "This garage is closed on Saturdays and will not be opened until Monday morning at 7am." WHAT? My car is in there! Today is Saturday! Why was the door open when I came if they are closed on Saturdays? I was so glad that Michelle waited to see if I was able to get in before leaving the scene. BUT Wait! This garage charged an hourly rate that would add up to several hundreds of dollars for the number of hours I would have to leave the car there!

Of course, over the weekend I was presented with all sorts of "what if's" and "If only's". OH! I thought about the fact that my husband was no longer alive. He would have taken care of a situation like this one. He was my anchor, my place of stability and security. I would always depend on him to make wrongs, right, and the crooked, strait! He would always fight for me. My father was always there to fight for me before I married. Now, who do I have to fight for me? I didn't know as much about God's care for widows then, as I know now.

I prayed desperately about that situation and told God that He had to go before me and fix this thing. I could not pay the amount of money that it would total! The entire weekend I prayed and confessed that God is a very present help in times of trouble. I even remember testifying to the congregation on that Sunday about the incident and I promised to give a victory report to them about Monday morning.

I made arrangements for Elder Ushry to pick me up from home early Monday morning and away we went to that downtown parking garage. WHEW! The garage door was open. Finally, I found someone to speak to concerning my dilemma. I had my argument all prepared as the man listened politely. "Is that your red vehicle over there?" He asked. "Yes! I answered, and continued to ask why the garage door was open Saturday, if they are supposed to be closed? I would not have driven in here if the doors were closed. How am I supposed to pay to get my car out of here? The man looked at me and said, "How much do you want to pay?" Gasping, I thought, "Well, I did use their facility". I replied by giving the very minimal amount. He said, Okay! And printed out a ticket for that amount. I drove to the cashier, paid the money and drove out of the garage. I told Elder Ushry that all was well. I praised the Lord all the way back home. Won't He Do It? HE SEES! HE KNOWS! HE CARES! I am now proud to say:

What a memorable manifestation of God's blessings upon this Widow!

ABOUT THE AUTHOR

Dr. Deborah J. Claxton is a third generation Christian and Baltimorean. She is one of sixteen children born to the late Bertram and Theresa Merritt. She received Jesus as Savior at 11 years of age.

FAMILY

► Wife of Chief Apostle Aaron B. Claxton over 60 years.
► Mother of seven children (3 daughters and 4 sons). Gayle, Bryan, Michael, Sharon, Michelle, David and Samuel
► Grandmother of 27, Great grandmother of 32
► Great-Great grandmother of 3

EDUCATION

► Graduate of Coppin State University-Baltimore, Maryland.
► Earned Masters' Degree from Johns Hopkins University.
► Received Doctor of Laws degree from Christian International Ministries.
► Received Doctor of Religious Education from Chesapeake Bible College and Seminary

MINISTRY / CAREER

- ► Taught in Baltimore City Public schools over 25 years.
- ► Taught parenting skills at the high school level.
- ► Served as a radio minister.
- ► Founded the Kinder-Rhema Day Care Center.
- ► Served with husband-pastor of New Creation Christian Church over 23 years.
- ► Founded the New Creation Christian Academy (1985).
- ► Has a global ministry and has taught and preached in Africa, Canada, Israel and in many cities across the US.
- ► Co-founder of The Deborah House Christian School, Aba, Nigeria, West Africa
- ► Founder and President of WWAM-Women With A Mission (A support ministry for women in leadership).
- ► Consecrated as an Apostle by Bishop Hamon, Christian International Ministries (2000)
- ► Now widowed but a "bride" waiting for her "Bridegroom"-"King of kings & Lord of lords."
- ► Writer & Author of the book entitled, "The Elect Lady".
- ► Books to be published, "Jesus, The Master Teacher," "The Lord is My Shepherd," "Facets of Salvation," "Suffer The Little Children," and "In My Father's House."

Her lifetime scripture:

Isaiah 59:21

"As for me, this is my covenant with them, saith the LORD; My spirit that is upon thee, and my word which I have put in thy mouth, shall not depart out of thy mouth, nor out of the mouth of thy seed, nor out of the mouth of thy seeds' seed, saith the LORD, from henceforth and forever."

Published Books by
Dr. Deborah J. Claxton & Chief Apostle Aaron B. Claxton:

Available Published Books written by Dr. Deborah J. Claxton:

► The Elect Lady

Available Published Books written by Chief Apostle Aaron B. Claxton:

► God's Plan for the Sons of Ham
► Beyond Sodom
► Possessing Our Earthy Inheritance Now
► First Fruits, the Missing Offering
► Understanding the Root, The Cause and the Remedy for the Middle East Conflict
► That Day Will Not Come Except

Contact information:
For information on how to obtain any of the above publications send your request to:
Dr. Deborah J. Claxton
Attn: Bookstore
P.O. Box 29180, Baltimore, Maryland, 21205
Email: info@ncccbalto.org | Phone# 410.488.5650

Books yet to be Published by Dr. Deborah J. Claxton:

► "The Lord Is My Shepherd"
► "Facets of Salvation"
► "Suffer the Little Children"
► "In My Father's House"
► "The Wonders of Widowhood" Volume 2

MOTIVATIONAL THOUGHTS & INSPIRATIONAL INSIGHTS

In addition to the books written, Dr. Claxton has demonstrated her God-given talent by writing on various subjects in poetic verse. Here is a sample:

- The Life!   The Lady!   The Legacy!
- If Only
- Learn Life
- Nine Ships Set Sailing!
- Well!   Well!   Well!
- Fascinating Perceptions

THE LIFE! THE LADY! THE LEGACY!
by Dr. Deborah J. Claxton

It was early on Thursday morning, February seventh,
Nineteen hundred thirty-five, in the year of our Lord; that I arrived.
Bertram and Theresa had started this blessed Merritt family;
And six other children had arrived before me.
There was Laverne, Telfair, Ruth, Naomi, Andre, and Timothy.

I don't know, but I was told that on the morning of my birth;
I could barely wait to make my appearance here on earth.
My Mom fell down a flight of steps, from the 2nd to the 1st floor;
As she was hastily preparing to go out of the front door.
My Dad picked her up and quickly put her into bed.
Hoping that the baby inside wasn't dead.
By the time the doctor arrived I was already here,
But I was taken to the hospital to avert any fear.

I suppose, God had a plan and Satan had one, too.
He thought, "Can't let her live, whatever I do.
Heard about this one before she left Heaven;
And guess what, demons, she's number seven!"

"So, what's so important about seven? Just tell me!
It's God's number of completion, perfection, and spirituality.
I'm afraid of her, I never know what might occur.
She and her angels always put me on the run;
And that's never, never, ever any fun!"

Well! Tell me, my friends, what more shall I say?
NOW! This Merritt household began prospering anyway.
"We need to move, this house is too small," one day, said her Dad.
So they moved from Franklin to Mount Street, and boy, were they glad!
"Our new house has three levels, a huge yard, and a cellar," Dad said with a grin;
So, we'll have plenty of space to grow and to expand within."
And expand they did with 9 more kids, sixteen of them in all;
And their God proved Himself faithful to minister to their need, beck and call.

Although, it wasn't long before some kinfolks moved in, too.
Uncle LaRoy, Aunt Helen, Mark, Paul, Lambert, Tyrone, and Gloria. WHEW!
Uncle LaRoy was the Pastor of the church we attended every Sunday;
Sometimes Wednesday, Friday and don't forget about Youth Night on Monday.
It was there we learned about God's wonderful redemption plan.
Readily available to every girl, boy, child, woman and man.
My brother, Timothy would preach to us siblings, every chance that he got,
He preached to us about Jesus, Heaven, and hell, whether we liked it or not.

Incidentally, Satan tried three more times to get rid of me;
But, he couldn't, you see, for God had already planned my destiny.

He tried with pneumonia, whooping cough, and a tumble down a
flight of stairs;
But I was covered by the BLOOD of Jesus, God's love, and all the
Saints' prayers.

During my last year of elementary school I surrendered to God's
call,
January, 1947, at the tender age of eleven, I said, "God, I want it
all!
I was baptized, tarried, and received the gift of the Holy Ghost!
I was glad, felt the joy and peace of the Lord, and began to make
my boast.
"The Creator of the universe, the Lord of Glory; He has set me
free!
If you are willing, He'll free you too, just like he did for me!
But my friends were not so happy. I received sneers and jeers.
They said, "A religious fanatic indeed!" There were some tears
and fears.
I did make it through high school and through my college years
as well.
I was motivated mainly by the Word of God and not wanting to
go to "hell."

As I began my teaching profession, I asked God for a suitable
mate;
I wanted to get married, before it was too late.
For through the years, I'd heard it preached, that Jesus could come
at any minute,
And in Heaven we live in spirit form, and there is no marriage in
it.

So God honored my cry, and sent me a guy, who was just what I'd
requested.
And this guy, Aaron Bobby Claxton, was also one in whom God
had invested.

So, we married each other in '58 and soon had seven children
between us.
It's more than sixty years later, and he has transitioned, and No! I
cannot fuss!

We've parented, traveled, preached, pastored, taught, loved, and
shared;
Pointing the way to life, hope, joy, and peace, showing that we
cared
About our 7 children, their mates, 34 grands, 36 great-grands, 3
great, great-grands, to-date;
Telling each generation, you're blessed; but make Jesus your
choice.
Don't let it be said, "Too late"!
There's a legacy that's been left on record for the generations to
come;
"You're blessed! You're favored! You're chosen by God! Each and
every one!"

IF ONLY
By Dr. Deborah J. Claxton

A WORD FROM THE LORD DURING COVID-19!

IF only during these "Unprecedented Times" you are willing
to "shut-in, shut-out and shut-up before the Lord, you will
spiritually move-up, chiefly because you will wise-up to what's-
up on God's agenda.

IF only during these times you would recognize that it's time for
a spiritual check-up so when it's time to go up, you'll be able to
robe-up in a garment of pure white.

IF only during these times you could understand that the Creator
has purposed to set-up the environment to help you to grow-up
in Him.

If only during these times you would give-up those things which
hinder, so that you will measure-up to God's righteous standard.

If only during these times you would study-up on the lives of
Peter, Paul and John, for it was when they were shut-up, that they
were charged-up, so that they could stand-up to any opposing
force.

IF only during these times you would not be reluctant to rise-up
to commune with your Redeemer, your Savior, your High Priest
and Friend, you would straighten-up, hold your head up and tear-
up, tear-down and terrorize satanic foes.

IF only during these times you would look-up and listen-up you
would hear God speak-up to show you clearly His way, His Word,
and His Will.

IF only during these "Unprecedented Times" you will read-up
on God's promises, your faith will blow-up fear, depression, and
doubt because your confidence will be built-up so there will be no
stopping you, NOW!

If only!   If Only!   IF ONLY!

LEARN LIFE
By Dr. Deborah J. Claxton

Life is a process, not a quick fix; it's a marathon with a sprint in
the mix!
Life moves! Life grows! Life matures! Life flows!
Life expands! Life develops! Life has a destiny!
Life was really meant to bless, to build, and keep you free!
Life has a beginning. Life comes to an end.
Life is for everyone whether foe or friend.

Life is a process, not a quick fix; it's a marathon with a sprint in
the mix!
Life is about times. Life is about seasons. It's about purpose and
reasons
Life is about nights and days, choices and ways.
Life is about heat. Life is about cold.
It's about summer and winter and memories foretold.
Life is about planting and reaping you see.
Life is for all – You were born free!
Life can make you happy, it can make you feel sad;
Sometimes it makes you feel down right mad.

Life is a process, not a quick fix; it's a marathon with a sprint in
the mix!
Life is very sure, it is not a guessing game;
Whether you're born in obscurity or gain national fame!
Life is a journey that begins when you're born, moving thru
various stages forlorn.
Anywhere along life's journey changes occur, that make the eyes
of your mind a blur.
Life is like a rose opening layer by layer;
But don't interrupt the process just to see what's hidden there!

Life is a process, not a quick fix; it's a marathon with a sprint in

the mix!
Life is a gift. Life is a packaged deal;
Meant to be enjoyed, to be treasured, to nurture, and appeal!
Life comes forth through struggle, that's a part of its making;
If not handled properly, struggle becomes life's breaking.
Life can be rich, life can be poor; this one thing about life is sure.
Life is made with built-in purpose to declare;
But you'll never be successful without focused prayer.

Life is a process, not a quick fix; it's a marathon with a sprint in
the mix!
However, inherent in life is death, we know not the day nor the
hour;
But Jesus took the sting out of death and it now has no power!
That is, to the ones who have been born again, forever in life to
reign!
The Designer of life has perfected the process; organized the
progress;
Gives strength in the distress; loves throughout the regress,
All the way to your success.

Life is a process, not a quick fix;
It's a marathon with a sprint in the mix!
SO YOU MUST LEARN LIFE!

[Motivated by a message from Dr. Myles Munroe]

NINE SHIPS SET SAILING!
By Dr. Deborah J. Claxton

Remember Noah? He built an ark.
Some may called it a boat; or how about a ship?
But, whatever you do, don't let these ships slip.
There are nine ships of success;
Those who miss these ships, usually end up in a mess.
Each one of these ships carries huge cargo in itself;
So, hop aboard! Don't ignore them! And don't think they're for
someone else.

The first one is "SONSHIP"
Just decide and say. "I'll take Jesus for mine."
The second one is "WORKMANSHIP."
Remember, God has already made you, Oh, so fine!
The third one is "FRIENDSHIP."
You'll need them, so choose your friends well!
The next is "FELLOWSHIP."
But don't follow the friends, who'll lead you to hell!
"SCHOLARSHIP" pays you in huge dividends;
And "RELATIONSHIP" supports you
Through the Church, your family and good friends.
Now everyone loves this other ship, you see;
They'll clap, shout and laugh – He-e, He-e, He-e;
It's "CHAMPIONSHIP", "Championship" Roar! Roar! Roar!
Championship has come to knock at your door.

Well! That's seven ships so far; what's the next one you say?
For the next ship, my friends, ask God and pray!
For this one you'll have to meditate hard and study long;
Because to get in this ship, you have to be strong.
Jesus got in; Chief Apostle and Bishop Bryan, too.
Pastor Sheila, and Dr. Deborah, just to name a few.
Those who have entered the other seven have a tip,

What is the name of this next ship? It is "LEADERSHIP"!
Eight ships of success, all ready to set sail, no doubt.
And Jesus sits interceding, so you won't be left out!
Now, it's time for 'WORSHIP'! Let's all give God a loud
HALLELUJAH shout!

WELL!   WELL!   WELL!
Inspired by Holy Spirit and written By Dr. Deborah J. Claxton

There was a Well, sitting on the well, waiting for a woman coming to draw water.

But the water in the well was not that WELL of water for which she really thirsted.

For the water in the well kept her coming to the well which did not satisfy.

But, by the time she finished drawing from that Well-of-Living Water;

Quenched, she left her waterpot there and ran back to the city.

Far and wide she spread the word; in all Samaria her voice was heard:

Saying, "Come see that WELL that was sitting on the well, who quenches the thirst of life."

She wanted everyone to know that the water from that WELL was the water they really craved.

For the water from this well is not the well from which to draw "Rivers of Living Water."

So, in masses they came to see and to hear; for two days they drew from that WELL.

Then, many more came to hear, drink, and be quenched from that WELL that had sat on the well.

After that, they went away quenched from the thirst for understanding of the mystery of the One to come – Jesus, the Messiah!

"Now we know for ourselves, they said with a frown, not just from that woman. Because!!

We drank for ourselves from that Living WELL, who sat on the well near our town."

FROM WHOSE WELL ARE YOU DRINKING and WHO'S DRINKING FROM YOUR WELL?
IS THERE A WELL OF WATER IN YOU SPRINGING UP INTO EVERLASTING LIFE?
Read St. John 4: 4-42; St. John 7: 37; Isa. 55: 1-13; Rev. 22: 1, 2

FASCINATING PERCEPTIONS
Inspired by the Late Dr. Myles Munroe and written by Dr. Deborah J. Claxton

The concealed God wants to rule the revealed world from the concealed world through the concealed Spirit living in the revealed body on the revealed earth.

Or

The invisible God wants to rule the visible world from the invisible world through the invisible Spirit living in the visible body on the visible earth.

Or

The unseen God wants to rule the seen world from the unseen world through the unseen Spirit living in the seen body on the seen earth.

Or
The supernatural God wants to rule the natural world from the supernatural world, through the supernatural spirit living in the natural body on the natural earth.

Pray

"Thy kingdom come; Thy will be done;
On earth as it is in Heaven."

So:
I said all of that to say, that:
"We walk by FAITH and not by SIGHT;
For the things that are SEEN are TEMPORAL;
But the things which are NOT SEEN are E-TER-NAL."

For without FAITH it is impossible to please GOD;
But, if we please GOD, He will bring us to that Promised Land
Which flows with "Milk" (natural benefits) and "Honey." (Sweet
pleasure) (II Cor. 5:7; 4: 18; Job 36:11, 12; Heb. 11:6)

CPSIA information can be obtained
at www.ICGtesting.com
Printed in the USA
LVHW040322250322
714342LV00002B/4